REFLECTIONS ON JESUS CHRIST

JACQUE LEONARD

Published 2025

Printed in the United States of America

First Edition

ISBN (softcover): 978-1-967842-35-3
ISBN (e-book): 978-1-967842-34-6

For information, address:

Holzer Books LLC
8 The Green, Ste. A
Dover, Delaware 19901 USA

For information about special discounts available for bulk purchases, sales promotions, and educational needs, contact:

info@holzerbooksllc.com
+1 (888) 901-7776

holzerbooksLLC©

CONTENTS

His Impact

PART I

Jesus the Christ

Christ, The Good Shepherd

Like the shepherd that leads
(And the sheep know his voice),
Is our Savior - the voice we can trust.
Do you know?
Can you hear?
Do you heed?

There are sheep that are lost
In this world full of woe;
They are His. They need help.
You He calls.
Do you know?
Can you hear?
Do you heed?

You can be His eyes as you hear His voice
You can find; you can reach; you can save.
He will lead us all as we heed His voice
Do you know?
Can you hear?
Do you heed?

As you heed His voice, He will help you lead.
You will know of the path you must take.
Through the valley so deep, through the mist and the fog
Grab the rod.
Grab a hand.
Heed His voice

John 10:11 I am the good shepherd; the good shepherd giveth his life for the sheep.

2

Christ's Mission

When the time for this Earth first came into God's plan,
The options were thought out with care.
When Adam and Eve made their choice to partake
The plan entered into this realm.

Firstborn of the Father, agreed to come down,
To give man a chance to go home.
Christ's mission was truly a mission of love,
Though the anguish He suffered was great.

He loved us His siblings enough to endure,
Ensure that the path home was cleared.
We've freedom to choose how we honor His love—
Accept it or turn clear away.

To honor His sacrifice, choose to go home,
Requires that we follow the plan:
Repent and obey while we serve as we're called,
Then look for a life in His world.

John 6:38 For I came down from heaven,
not to do mine own will, but the will of him that sent me.

Jesus Christ: Comforter

At times of lowest lows,
When life around us flows,
And all seems dark and drear...

That's when our Savior's near.

His comfort he'll avail
To all outside the veil.
Those who will humbly kneel-

Their broken hearts He'll heal.

He'll take on Him our load,
His peace on us bestowed.
His promise is our bond;

He'll help us go beyond.
We simply must look up,
To move from us the cup
That threatens to o'ertake.

Just reach—
— the contact make.

John 14:18-19 I will not leave you comfortless; I will come to you. Yet a little while, and the world seeth me no more; but ye see me: because I live, ye shall live also.

"As even a small lamp brings a light to our path through the night, Jesus Christ brings His Light to the World."

JESUS CHRIST:
LIGHT OF THE WORLD

When Jesus spent time on this earth, He was Light.
He showed us just how to shine forth with His might.
He taught us to reach out, and serve one and all.
Let's heed Him, and reach out, and answer His call.

We do what He taught in our homes, in our world;
The poor and the needy, safe in our arms curled.
When life treats us harshly, we count on His aid.
Thus strengthened, we shine, never really afraid.

It takes courage to live our lives just as He taught.
Oft times, it's not easy when life leaves us naught.
We trust Him. We know Him. He gives us great strength.
His light thus shines through us; we'll go to great length.

To let Him shine through us begins when we know.
We've studied and prayed; we've asked Him how to grow.
To act means our curtains let all His light shine;
Becoming a pathway for His force divine.

John 8:12 Then spake Jesus again unto them, saying, I am the light of the world: he that followeth me shall not walk in darkness, but shall have the light of life.

Our Advocate

At times in our lives, we can feel very small,
As if all that we are, doesn't matter at all.
Occasions comes up that require much more;
When we've nothing at all that will serve in our store.

It's then we've a need for a lawyer to plead,
To take on the hard task, else we surely will bleed.
No way, on our own, can we answer the call;
For we never could win, though we'd give it our all.

We can't enter heaven, despite all our work.
Though we strive to be righteous and seldom do shirk.
Because we're not perfect, despite our travail,
A great advocate's needed for help through the veil.

He knows us. He loves us. He makes us like new.
Yes, he's ever our advocate, helping us through.
He only requires us to stay on the path.
Thus we love Him and serve Him, receive all he Hath.

1 John 2:1 My little children, these things write I unto you, that ye sin not: And if any man sin, we have an advocate with the Father, Jesus Christ the righteous.

The Messiah,
the Anointed One

Our Christ is the Messiah,
Anointed as a Prophet.
To help us find our way;
He gives light, lest we should stray.

Our Christ is the Messiah,
Anointed as a Priest.
To tend to each day's trials,
He gives succor through the miles.

Our Christ is the Messiah,
Anointed as a King.
To lead with strong defenses,
He always right dispenses.

Our Christ is the Messiah,
Anointed as a Deliverer.
To save us from our errors,
He rescues us from terrors.

Our Christ is the Messiah,
Anointed as our Lord
To shepherd with His watch-care,
He answers every prayer.

Luke 4:18 The Spirit of the Lord is upon me, because he hath anointed me to preach the gospel to the poor; he hath sent me to heal the brokenhearted, to preach deliverance to the captives, and recovering of sight to the blind, to set at liberty them that are bruised.

THE ONLY BEGOTTEN SON

Just what do we know of this man we call Christ?
The answer is open to all.
He wants us to know; it's not hidden from view.
His mission requires us to know.

His mother was Mary, a virgin quite pure.
His Father, divine from on high.
He lived as a man, though with never a sin;
The Only Begotten on earth.

He lay down His life and then took it back up.
He taught us that we, too, can rise.
Yes, all we must do is believe and be true,
Repent and then move towards the goal.

To gain strength to follow His path is our quest,
It happens one choice at a time.
Begin each new day with a prayer on our lips,
Commune oft throughout all our trials.

Our choice is to know Him and follow His path.
He's shown us the way to proceed.
He is, so we may through His grace yet become.
He'll lead us and show us the way.

1 John 4:9 In this was manifested the love of God toward us, because that God sent his only begotten Son into the world, that we might live through him.

9

Jesus Christ:
The Bread of Life

A basic truth, bread giveth life
And hath through times long past.
Our Christ has taught that He gives life
Like bread, and so He does.

When bread we eat, we soon need more.
With Christ, that's not the case.
Believe and live forevermore
So basic, yet so hard.

In some small part, we know it's true.
We love both bread and Christ.
We study scriptures through and through
And have one hunger met.

We savor, taste a fresh baked bread,
And deep inside we smile.
It satisfies a soul-deep thread,
That ties us to this earth.

Yes, Christ gives life, we know it's true.
Though bread is comfort food,
Our greatest comfort through and through
Is Christ, deep in our core.

John 6:35 And Jesus said unto them. I am the bread of life: he that cometh to me shall never hunger; and he that believeth in me shall never thirst.

WITHOUT SIN

Our Savior had a mortal Mom
Who pondered o'er her son:
In ways, he grew as any boy,
Yet He was more, the only One.

The only One who never sinned,
Obedience was His way.
He e'er obeyed His Father's will.
Their will was one, He'd say.

He taught and lived the perfect life,
In every way a man.
His life was short, yet full enough,
To follow Heavenly Father's plan.

Because He lived and died for us,
We have a chance to soar.
He paid the price for all our sins,
So we can live, forevermore.

1 Peter 2:21-22 For even hereunto were ye called: because Christ also suffered for us, leaving us an example, that ye should follow his steps: Who did no sin, neither was guile found in his mouth.

PART II
His Life

REJOICE IN THE ATONEMENT OF CHRIST

Music by: Jacque Leonard

Lyrics by: Jacque Leonard

Arranged by: Jacque Leonard

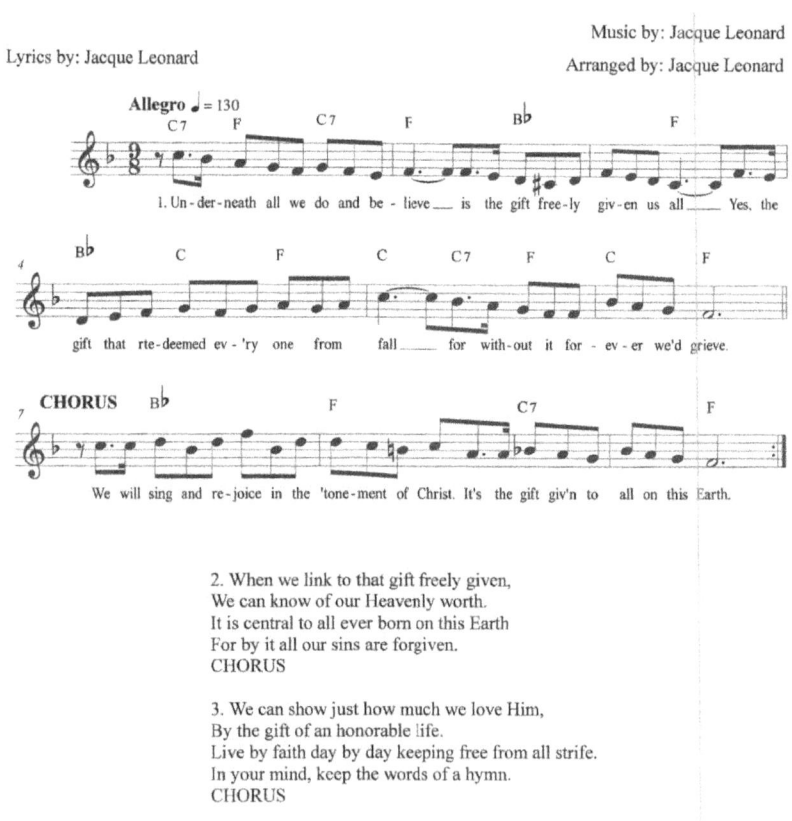

2. When we link to that gift freely given,
We can know of our Heavenly worth.
It is central to all ever born on this Earth
For by it all our sins are forgiven.
CHORUS

3. We can show just how much we love Him,
By the gift of an honorable life.
Live by faith day by day keeping free from all strife.
In your mind, keep the words of a hymn.
CHORUS

Romans 5:11 And not only so, but we also joy in God through our Lord Jesus Christ, by whom we have now received the atonement.

THE THREADS OF LIFE

Lyrics and Music by Jacque Leonard

♩ = 108

1. Through the thoughts and ac - tions day by day We weave the fab - ric of our life So - me thoughts and acts leave threads of white A - nd some lea - ve streaks o - f dark - e - st gray

Chorus
We must weave the fa - br - ic of o - ur life and choose just the threads that are whit - e - st white.

2. As we think and ponder on that cloth
And recognize the pattern there,
We may have cause to morn the gray
And look upon our life with wroth.
Chorus

3. There's a way for us to change the weave,
And make it intricate and pure.
As He who made us did intend.
Then we will not have cause to grieve.
Chorus

4. We must pull all threads of darkest hue.
Must pull them one by one by one.
Repent the path that put them there,
Then weave in threads that we'll not rue.
Chorus

5. Yes, Our Lord has shown us all the light.
He's paid the price for all our sin.
When we repent, we honor Him.
We'll live with Him in whitest white.
Chorus

**I Corinthians 9:17 For I do this thing willingly, I have a reward:
but if against my will, a dispensation of the gospel is committed unto me.**

15

CHRIST, OUR EXEMPLAR

When deep down inside us we're feeling a need
To know how to act, how to heal when we bleed-
The world gives us books and has answers galore,
Our Savior can offer us more, so much more.

He is the Exemplar, He's shown us the way,
And through His atonement we'll see Him some day.
That hope gives us reason to follow His path,
To reach out to others and earn Satan's wrath.

We need to give love and to feel it within.
We need to stay faithful, avoid calls to sin,
To search out the scriptures and heed Spirit's call,
He's opened the way for the one and the all.

No need to be lonely, to bleed from our wounds.
No need to feel lost and abandoned, marooned.
Christ is our Exemplar, He's shown us the way,
And through His atonement we'll see Him some day.

*1 Peter 2:21 For even hereunto were ye called: because Christ also suffered for us,
leaving us an example, that ye should follow his steps.*

THE WAY

Endlessly patient, long-suffering was He,
As He pushed through the crowd on His way.
He was touched by a woman who longed to be whole.
By her faith she was healed in that day.

Know that, with patience, our prayers will be heard.
We move forth but we wait for His aid.
Though it's hard, we pray on and we know that he hears
It's what's best that we'll get— ne'er betrayed.

Choice He has granted to each of His own.
How we use it foretells how we'll fare.
We can turn from all others or be as His hands,
We can listen or choose not to care.

Suffering's the lot of so many we know,
There are blessings when quietly endured.
We may find ourselves lifted when rendering aid.
And we will, when we've finally matured.

Truly Christ showed us the path we should take,
As we learn to have patience within.
Though we suffer through life, suffering helps us to grow.
Bitter shows us the sweet; thanks to Him.

Luke 8:43-44 And a woman having an issue of blood twelve years, which had spent all her living upon physicians, neither could be healed of any, Came behind him and touched the border of his garment: and immediately her issue of blood stanched.

THE ENABLING POWER
OF JESUS CHRIST

Are you feeling quite weak with the struggles you face?
Does it feel like you're bound tight and trapped?
In the Scriptures are stories of lives you can trace,
Yet their truths will not make you feel strapped.

They all point to a Father who fashioned this earth,
As a place for His children to learn.
His love gave to them lessons they'd need from their birth,
So they'd know how His presence they'd earn.

For He gave us His Son to show mankind the way,
And to pay for our sins with His life.
We've been gifted His strength as we go on our way,
He will help us to overcome strife.

Can you shut down your pride and admit that you're weak?
Can you trust Him to lend you His strength?
He will help you or show you, when His help you seek.
For His arms have no limited length.

Read the stories that show, when we follow His path,
How He helps and supports and saves lives.
Those who torment His own will be shown His great wrath,
He assures that their plan never thrives.

Yes, your Heavenly Father's enabled your way,
He's provided a path to His home.
Read the stories that show, spend some time every day—
Soon you'll chose never more for to roam.

John 13:15 I have given you an example that ye should do as I have done.

CHARITY

Charity's more than the things that you do;
Part of it's seeing the good around you,
Seeing the hand of the Lord in your world,
Glorious creation, the Heavens round you swirled.
Your feelings of joy and your wanting to share,
The Lord's acts of mercy, His answers to prayer,

Gifts He has given so freely to you,
Gifts like your loved ones, His great mercy, too.
All of these gifts showered down from above,
Add to the wonderful gift of His love;
That ultimate gift, yes, the gift of His Son,
Atonement for all of the wrongs that you've done.

Charity's more than just something you give.
Down deep inside, choose just how you will live.
Let it be part of the good that you are.
Learn not to judge; let your love reach out far.
Accept all the differences, shortcomings, too.
Let no one offend you; forgive what they do.

Charity's part of your everyday life,
Children and teenagers kept free from strife,
Those in your lives whose perfection you aid,
Challenge your thoughts toward the choices you've made.
It matters. It matters much more than you know,
For charity starts in the home where it grows.

Peace is bestowed on you when you are true;
Charity guides all the things that you do.
When you let charity transform your heart,
You become like Him; you're doing your part.
The Pure love of Christ can be deep in your soul,
It's one of life's pleasures, not some lofty goal.

1 Corinthians 13:4 Charity suffereth long, and is kind; charity envieth not; charity vaunteth not itself, is not puffed up,....Charity never faileth.

GIFT AS JESUS GIVES

Music by: I. Reed Payne

Lyrics by: Jacque Leonard
Arranged by: Jacque Leonard

2. What joy can come into our lives when our gifts show His heart?
Can we seek out a different way to better play our part?
Perhaps this is the Christmas a far better way to start.
Let's act as if we, all of us, had deep in us His heart.

3. To follow His example in the gift we choose to give,
Sometimes it simply means that others hurts we must forgive.
Sometimes we must reach out with love that other souls might live.
This Chrismas time reach out with thought and gift as Jesus gives.

*Matthew 18:35 So likewise shall my heavenly father do also unto you,
if ye from your hearts forgive not every one his brother their trespasses.*

Doctrines of the Heart

In a church, in a church, in a Christ-Centered church,
The parents are taught and their teaching enhanced.
In a church, in a church, in a Christ Centered Church
Poor training is not to be chanced.

In a home, in a home, in a Gospel-filled home,
The doctrines are shared with strong feelings of love.
In a home, in a home, in a Gospel home
You can feel the Spirit from above.

In a soul, in a soul, in a heaven-bound soul,
All the doctrines ring true as they're learned.
In a soul, in a soul, in a heaven-bound soul
Seeds of truth will not often be spurned.

In a heart, in a heart, in a true Christ-like heart,
There's a need to reach out and to share.
In a heart, in a heart, in a true Christ-like heart,
His great strength, it will ever be there.

Nehemiah 9:20 Thou gavest also thy good spirit to instruct them,
and withholdest not thy manna from their mouth, and gavest them water for their thirst.

BUILDING FAITH
IN THE LORD JESUS CHRIST

How can we build a firm Faith in the Lord
That teaches, protects and sustains?
How do we take the most precious dear Soul,
And carefully nurture the flames?

How do we know of the hurt deep inside,
That many are hiding from view?
How can we help do the work of the Lord?
Just what does He want us to do?

Here is the plan that was carefully laid
To reach every person in need.
Join every person in households of faith,
And call those of faith to the lead.

Organize people and teach them to serve.
Each month plan a visit with love.
Teach them to pray as they walk side-by-side
Toward light from the heavens above.

Hear the word spoken and written each week.
Let words sink down deep in each heart
Foster true righteousness deep in each soul
And pray. Ask in faith. Do your part.

Faith will be built through consistent firm steps;
That path will lead people back home.
People all over the world will rejoice,
For Faith will bring everyone HOME.

Romans 10:17 So then faith cometh by hearing, and hearing by the word of God.

Faith Leads
to a Feeling of Love

Are you feeling a need to know more of His love?
Do you want to have blessings show'red down from above?
Well, then I have a gift, and I'll give it to you.
For I'll tell you the things you should pray and should do.

Here's this small tiny seed for to plant in your soul.
Now we'll plant it down deep in this small little hole,
Yes, this hole in your heart that's been leaking for years.
Then we'll let it grow there - so hush, calm down those fears.

Can you feel it beginning to grow in your soul?
Now don't you dig it up, that is just not your role;
For your job is to nurture it— help it to grow.
And have faith that this seed it is good, soon you'll know.

Can you feel it beginning to lighten your mind?
Have you noticed you want to be nothing but kind?
So delicious to feel and to know and to have,
This small plant to your soul has become quite a salve.

When you prayed for some help for to heal up your hole,
Our kind Father sent others to help mend your soul.
He sent you that small seed of faith, just for you.
And you planted it, nurtured it, helped it grow, too.

Now you know that God loves you, and that is enough
I'm not saying that life won't be sad, won't be tough.
For you know that He loves you, you trust in His care;
All your burdens are lifted for He's always there.

Luke 8:11 Now the parable is this: the seed is the word of God.

OBEDIENCE

As we ponder the life of our Savior,
We can find an example to follow;
For He did as His Father requested,
An example obedient behavior.

And just why should we ponder obedience?
For what gain could we possibly find there?
But there's wisdom to come in the quiet,
When we throw out our personal defiance.

When we study His word and revere it,
When we strive to live just as He taught us,
Then there's answers and peace for us daily,
As we strive to forever be near it.

For He gave us His word and example,
And He showed us the winding road home.
So we study and follow Him daily,
And we find our reward more than ample.

Deuteronomy 4:40 Thou shalt keep therefore his statutes, and his commandments, which I command thee this day, That it may go well with thee, and with thy children after thee, and that thou mayest prolong thy days upon the earth, which the Lord thy God giveth thee, forever.

CHRISTLIKE LOVE

When we reach to others with His Christ-like love,
When we are the arms of our Father above,
When we can encourage and strengthen and serve,
When we heed the Spirit and we do not swerve,
Then we know the meaning of Charity.

Real, true love's not what we give away,
It's what we acquire; it's just part of our way.
We're never the same when it plants in our heart,
For judgment and sniping are no more our part-
When we know the meaning of Charity.

We forgive everyone who has caused us a hurt,
Refuse to spread even a wee bit of dirt.
We look for the best in each beautiful soul,
And pray for their hurt that they may be whole,
For we are the essence of Charity.

Let's say when there's need, "Here I am, please send me."
As Christ led the way for all people to see,
Th' Atonement - the ultimate Charity act.
He laid down His life and completed His pact.
Christ's Love is the heart of our Charity.

*John 6:38 For I came down from heaven, not to do mine own will,
but the will of him that sent me.*

PART IV

His Impact

THE LORD'S TENDER MERCIES

Music and Lyrics by Jacque Leonard

1. Do the Lord's ten-der mer-cies seem dis-tant and far? Does it seem that the Lord does-n't know who you are? Are you weighed down with cares of a dif-fi-cult life? Is your home filled with ten-sion, dis-or-der and strife?

Chorus

The Lord wants to show-er His bless-ings on you, ten-der mer-cies are wait-ing for you. Ten-der mer-cies to car-ry you all your life through. Just seek and you'll find them come in-to your view.

Tenor solo as an alternate chorus or ending

Will you let me come in-to your life? Will you o-pen your heart when I knock? Let me love you and lift up your load? Ten-der mer-cies I'd bring to your life!

2. What if you answered yes to the questions above?
Does that mean you will ne'er feel the peace of His love?
Well, there's blessed assurance that needn't be true.
For the Lord's tender mercies are waiting for you.

3. Our God doesn't have favorites on some special list.
For life isn't a lottery whose numbers you've missed.
In our hearts, our obediece the Lord seeks to find.
Just what is it you hope for, what thoughts fill your mind?

4. It's your job to choose Him and follow His lead.
And then He's free to shower His love on your need.
He'll speak peace to your soul and give comfort and aid,
For He loves you; the price of your sins He has paid.

5. Yes, the Lord's tender mercies are waiting for you,
For the Lord knows your heart, all the things that you do.
He will take on your burdens, life needn't be dire,
If you'll open your heart to the Holy Ghost's fire.

James 5:11 Behold, we count them happy which endure. Ye have heard of the patience of Job, and have seen the end of the Lord, that the Lord is very pitiful, and of tender mercy.

BECAUSE

Because a virgin pure and good,
Accepted Divine Motherhood
He lived.

Because He did as Father bid,
His light He never, never hid,
We know.

Because He loved us as His own,
He taught us all that we are known.
He cares.

Because He died, we all can live.
We do our best, we share and give.
He helps.

Because it is our Father's Way
We'll live with Him again someday.
Give Thanks!

John 10:28 And I give unto them eternal life; and they shall never perish, neither shall any man pluck them out of my hand.

THE LOVE OF THE LORD

Oh, to feel of the love of The Lord in our lives!
'Tis a gift that all people who've felt of this love
Will want for each one on this planet to know.
They've no wish for to ever forget.

Is it possible any could feel such a thing?
If they could, oh how loudly their heartstrings would sing
Earthly leaders have told us that we, too, can feel,
If we'd change just a few simple things.

When you feel of His love, feel His arms 'round your soul,
You feel strong; you feel power; you can conquer the world.
For you have no desire to step off of path.
It's the path to your heavenly home.

When you love in return, that is when you're complete.
For your virtue's intact, and your character strong.
Yes you want to do right both in day and in night.
You are loved and you love in return.

If you've not felt this love, there is much you might do
For you'll all want to feel His strong arms around you.
Start by keeping a journal of blessings you know
There give thanks for the good in your life

This will lead you to Him, and to all that He is.
He's the source of all good, so you'll feel of His love.
Because this is a gift, and it's offered to you,
When you seek Him in all that you do.

For this gift of His love will propel you to good.
It will motivate you in the things that you do.
Then you'll want to remove all that's wrong from your life,
And to bridle your passions each day.

When you live such a life, so complete and so full,
It is never enough to just know that He cares
Open up and then feel it down deep in your soul.
It's His gift, yes His life changing gift,

And He's given it all, just for you!

Acts 2:28 Thou hast made known to me the ways of life;
thou shalt make me full of joy with thy countenance.

CHRIST'S POWER'S THERE FOR ME

If He had power to form the Earth and everything therein,
If He had power to raise the dead and pay the price for sins,
If He had power to feed the crowds and calm the angry sea,
If He had power to rise again, then there's enough for me.

He asks that I repent each day and strive to follow right.
He asks that I beseech in prayer quite constant, day and night.
He asks that I seek out His lambs and help them find the fold.
He asks that I continue on with rod firm in my hold.

Because He has the power to form the Earth and all therein,
Because He has the power to raise the dead and pay for sins,
Because He has the power to feed the crowds and calm the sea,
Because He has the power to rise again, there's hope for me.

I have the power to repent and strive to follow right.
I have the power to pray to Him each morning, noon and night.
I have the power to seek His lambs and help them find the fold.
I have the power to forward move, with rod within my hold.

He has the power to save me and to bring me safely home.
To Him belongs the glory for now and evermore.

Acts 1:8 But ye shall receive power, after that the Holy Ghost is come upon you: and ye shall be witnesses unto me both in Jerusalem, and in all Judaea, and in Samaria, and unto the uttermost part of the earth.

WITHOUT GUILE

To never intend to do anyone harm,
To be without guile in the world-
How oft do we manage to live as He taught,
Just loving and giving and pure?

Each day we repent, and we try yet again,
To live as we know He desires.
To say we believe, but to live the world's way?
Hypocrisy, darkening our path.

Christ showed us the way with the choices He made.
Each day we can choose our own way.
We follow the path that He showed with His life,
We know He smiles down on His own.

1 Peter 2:22 Who did no sin, neither was guile found in his mouth.

PREPARING THE WAY

There is coming a day when The Lord will return.
What can we do to prepare?
Are there skills on this earth that we yet need to learn?
Knowledge we still need to share?

While it's true that He's coming, we don't know the day,
Trouble and changes are sure.
We're just called to be righteous in every way,
Strong— with a heart that is pure.

When we make a mistake, we'll repent right away.
Friendship will show that we're true.
We'll show others the path, as we live in this way,
Faithful in all that we do.

We have learned there's a way to lead others to Him.
Be all we know how to be.
Live by standards; don't let them grow dim.
Start every day on our knees.

When we live in this way, in that day we'll rejoice;
Secure in our mansions on high.
His atonement makes up for our shortfalls in choice;
Give thanks that His coming is nigh!

Luke 1:17 And he shall go before him in the Spirit and power of Elias, to turn the hearts of the fathers to the children, and the disobedient to the wisdom of the just; to make ready a people prepared for the Lord.

Jacque Leonard was born in Coeur d'Alene, Idaho in 1945. The career of her choice even as a child, was to be a teacher. She attended Whitworth University in Spokane, Washington, received her Bachelor's degree in 1967, got married and moved to southern California. There she continued her education becoming certified in multiple arenas including Special Education. Jacque has always had a busy creative mind. She loves music, singing, playing her cello, and eventually composing music of her own. She has always loved words. She is a veracious reader in multiple genres. She began writing poetry while in college and has written over 140 poems. She is a Distinguished Toastmaster and loves to speak competitively. Her teaching has touched lives of all ages. In the public schools she taught every age from preschool to high school. She has trained teachers and traveled for 17 years as a corporate trainer.

She and her husband have two children and four grandchildren. They are currently living in Northern Idaho, near where Jacque was born. Their daughter lives with them helping care for their home and puppy. They are active in their religious faith. Their son lives in Utah with his wife. Their four grandchildren's lives are based near them.

Rachel Rounsville Christensen (b. 1996) is a representational realist artist specializing in figurative painting and impressionist landscapes. After receiving a Bachelors of Art from Brigham Young University in 2019, she pursued training in representational drawing and painting by apprenticing under master artists Patricia McMahon Rice, Susan Lyon, and Casey Childs. She's been recognized by the Portrait Society of America and Southwest Art Magazine's 21 Under 31: Young Artists to Collect Now as an up-and-coming artist and her work has been included in exhibitions across the US. As she's traveled throughout the world and lived in different communities, Rachel's art has been inspired by the incredible people she's encountered and the way they shape the natural world around them. She currently resides in San Clemente, California with her young family.

www.ingramcontent.com/pod-product-compliance
Lightning Source LLC
Chambersburg PA
CBHW051248120626
46547CB00014B/1841